Original title:

Unified Echoes

Author: Swan Charm

ISBN HARDBACK: 978-1-80560-052-7

ISBN PAPERBACK: 978-1-80560-517-1

Harmonizing Echoes

In the grove where silence sings,
Whispers dance on gentle wings,
Nature's breath an echo clear,
Every note, a love so dear.

Moonlight filters through the trees,
Swaying softly in the breeze,
Stars aligned in perfect tune,
Harmonies beneath the moon.

Rivers sing their ancient song,
Flowing sweetly, never wrong,
In the night, where shadows play,
Melodies of night and day.

Footsteps tracing paths anew,
Every step a rhythm true,
Chasing echoes, vast and wide,
In this echo, hearts abide.

Voices merge in twilight's glow,
Threads of sound begin to flow,
Together in this sacred space,
Harmonizing time and place.

Melodies in Silence

In the stillness, whispers bloom,
Echoed thoughts in gentle room.
Shadows dance in soft embrace,
Harmony wrapped in quiet space.

Unseen notes begin to rise,
Carrying dreams, like silent sighs.
Every heartbeat plays its part,
Melody born from the heart.

A hush that holds the world at bay,
Guiding souls in a tender sway.
In the silence, secrets dwell,
Unfolding tales no words can tell.

Stars above, a cosmic tune,
Playing softly to the moon.
In the quiet, love ignites,
Melodies of endless nights.

Together in this sacred place,
Finding peace in slowest pace.
Melodies echo, soft and bright,
In the silence, we find light.

Collective Reverberations

Voices rise in harmony,
Bound together, wild and free.
Echos form a vibrant blend,
In unity, we transcend.

Rhythms dance through every vein,
Shared emotions, joy and pain.
Collective strength, we stand tall,
Together we can conquer all.

Notes arise, a choir strong,
Symphonies weave where we belong.
In the reverberate of sound,
A deeper truth can be found.

Heartbeat syncing, pulse in line,
Each breath shared, a sacred sign.
Together we create the tune,
Brightening the darkest noon.

Through waves of sound, our hearts entwine,
An endless melody divine.
In every note, we find our way,
Collective reverberations stay.

Tides of Togetherness

Waves of laughter crash ashore,
Binding hearts forevermore.
Every moment, tides that swell,
In this bond, all is well.

Underneath the starlit sky,
Together, we learn to fly.
In these currents, we are one,
Chasing dreams 'til day is done.

Like the tide that ebbs and flows,
Through the storms, our love still grows.
United, we weather all fate,
Trusting in what we create.

Hand in hand, we build our way,
Guided by the light of day.
Even when the oceans roar,
We stand firm, we are the shore.

In every tide, there's strength anew,
Together facing skies so blue.
In the rhythm, we find grace,
Tides of togetherness embrace.

Symphonic Reflections

Mirrors shatter into sound,
Echoes of hope all around.
In reflections, truths appear,
Symphonic whispers crystal clear.

Notes collide and spark a flame,
Every heart plays in this game.
Resonance of dreams we chase,
In this space, we find our place.

Harmonies of joy and pain,
Through our losses, we gain.
Each reflection tells a story,
In symphonies, we find glory.

Through the depths, our spirits rise,
Painting colors in the skies.
Every chord reveals our theme,
In this symphony, we dream.

Together in this grand design,
Tuning into love's pure line.
In reflections, we unite,
Symphonic echoes, pure delight.

Connected Resonance

In the quiet of the night,
Whispers of stars ignite.
Threads of the past unwind,
Echoes through space combined.

Every heartbeat's a song,
Creating bonds so strong.
Like rivers that intertwine,
Our souls in dance align.

Moments we cannot see,
Shape our shared history.
With each tremor we feel,
The universe becomes real.

In the fabric of time,
Love is the perfect rhyme.
Connected through the light,
We shine in endless night.

Together we explore,
What we have yearned for.
Resonating with grace,
In this vast, boundless space.

Threads of Synchronicity

In the tapestry of fate,
Every stitch resonates.
Moments align like threads,
Guiding where life spreads.

The dance of chance unfolds,
In stories yet untold.
Paths crossing, fate's embrace,
Infinite time and space.

Dreams weave a subtle tune,
Beneath the silver moon.
When hearts begin to see,
How deep our bonds can be.

With each whisper of the wind,
A new journey begins.
In rhythm, we find peace,
Through love, our souls release.

United in this flow,
Together, we will grow.
In synchronicity's glow,
We share what we both know.

Harmonizing Hearts

In the symphony of life,
Where joy blends with strife.
Each heartbeat plays a part,
Creating art from the heart.

Melodies softly rise,
Under expansive skies.
Together we compose,
A world where love flows.

Chords of laughter ring clear,
Echoing far and near.
In this grand design,
We find the joy divine.

With hands held side by side,
In harmony, we glide.
Every note we create,
Inspires love's warm fate.

In the music we share,
There's magic in the air.
Hearts syncing as we play,
Together, come what may.

Chorus of the Cosmos

Underneath vast starlit skies,
Wonders and secrets arise.
In the chorus of night,
We find our shared light.

Galaxies spin and twirl,
In a timeless swirl.
Singing galaxies call,
Uniting us, one and all.

Constellations align,
In patterns so divine.
Each twinkle, a reminder,
Of love that pulls us wider.

In the depths of the void,
Dreams and hopes are enjoyed.
Together, we align,
In a dance so fine.

As the universe sings,
Hope in every heart springs.
In this cosmic embrace,
We find our rightful place.

Unity in Sound

In the whisper of the breeze,
Voices of many unite,
A melody that is free,
Dancing hearts in the light.

In the rhythm of the rain,
Each drop sings a sweet tune,
Harmony flows through the pain,
A symphony 'neath the moon.

From the mountains to the sea,
Nature weaves its soft thread,
Together we all can be,
In this song, we are led.

Every note is a story,
Each chord a life lived well,
In our shared glory,
We find peace, we dwell.

A chorus of silent hearts,
Echoing through the years,
Together, never apart,
Unity quells our fears.

Cadence of the Whole

Each step in the dance we take,
Brings us closer to our fate,
In the rhythm of our wake,
Harmony we create.

The pulse of life in our veins,
Beats in time with the earth,
In the joy and the pains,
We find our true worth.

With every rise and the fall,
We weave the thread of our days,
In the silence, we hear the call,
In the beauty, we praise.

From dawn till the end of night,
We shall dance in delight,
Finding strength in our plight,
Together, we shine bright.

The cadence of the whole,
Resonates through the crowd,
In the rhythm of the soul,
We sing out loud!

Echos of the Ancients

In the shadows of the past,
Lies a wisdom so deep,
Through the ages it will last,
In our hearts, we must keep.

Voices whisper in the trees,
Stories of what has been,
In the rustle of the leaves,
Echoes of lives we've seen.

Ancient songs within our blood,
Flow like rivers of gold,
In the rhythm of each flood,
Tales of courage unfold.

Through the trials we have faced,
Strength has woven our fate,
In this journey, we're embraced,
Bound by love, never late.

Let the echoes guide our way,
To the future we create,
In their wisdom, we shall stay,
Finding peace in our fate.

Entwined Harmonies

In the garden of our dreams,
Flowers bloom side by side,
Entwined in sunlit beams,
With nature as our guide.

Joined by roots, we are strong,
Each petal tells a tale,
In this chorus, we belong,
Together we shall sail.

Through the seasons of our lives,
We dance with joy and pain,
In our hearts, the music thrives,
In the sun and the rain.

With each note, we lift our voice,
Celebrating what we share,
In this moment, we rejoice,
A tapestry so rare.

Unified, our spirits soar,
In the harmony we bring,
Forever we will explore,
As one, we are the spring.

The Dance of Resonance

In shadows soft, we meet tonight,
Our whispers weave, a tapestry bright.
With every step, the world fades away,
Two souls entwined in a rhythmic sway.

The moon above, a guiding light,
Reflecting dreams that take their flight.
We sway to a song only we know,
In this embrace, our passions grow.

A heartbeat echoes, the tempo swells,
In this union, no one tells.
The music flows, a sacred stream,
Each note a wish, each glance a dream.

Fingers lace, in motion divine,
Through the night, our spirits entwine.
In every twirl, the silence breaks,
A symphony of love, our hearts awake.

As dawn approaches, the dance must end,
Yet in each step, our dreams transcend.
We'll carry this rhythm, forever bold,
In the dance of life, our story unfolds.

Unbroken Cadence

With every beat, the ground vibrates,
We move as one, defying fates.
In perfect harmony, our voices rise,
Echoes weaving through the skies.

A steady pulse, our hearts aligned,
In the stillness, love's defined.
We step in sync, through fire and rain,
Building a bridge from joy and pain.

Unbroken cadence, a vital thread,
We dance through moments, both unsaid.
A powerful call, through shadows long,
Together we forge our unyielding song.

The world may shake, the storms may clash,
Yet in this rhythm, we shall not crash.
Our spirits rise, unbound by fate,
In this unbroken, we resonate.

With every dawn, new steps await,
Shaped by trials, love will not wait.
Through every heartbeat and silent cheer,
We carry our song, forever near.

Echoing Hearts

In the quiet of the night, we rendezvous,
With words unspoken, our hearts anew.
Melodies linger, sweet and pure,
In the depths of silence, love will endure.

Faint echoes drift through the air,
Each whisper a promise, a love we share.
Together we find the pulse of our soul,
In hearts entwined, we become whole.

A symphony rises, each note divine,
With every glance, our spirits align.
The rhythm of time softly weaves,
In the fabric of night, our story believes.

Through valleys low, and mountains high,
In harmony's arms, we learn to fly.
Echoing laughter, dance of the free,
In every heartbeat, you're part of me.

As twilight fades, the stars ignite,
Guiding our hearts through the endless night.
Bound by the music of this sacred art,
Together forever, echoing hearts.

Communal Songs

Gathered around where our spirits meet,
Stories unfold in a gentle beat.
Voices rise in a vibrant throng,
In this circle, we've found our song.

Hands held tight, we share the fire,
With every laugh, we lift higher.
A tapestry woven from dreams and fears,
In the warmth of love, we shed our tears.

Communal songs of strength and grace,
In every rhythm, we find our place.
The cadence flows as memories blend,
Each note a bond that will not end.

Through dusk and dawn, in sun or rain,
We sing together through joy and pain.
An unbroken chain, a sacred trust,
In these verses, we rise, we must.

As seasons change and time flows on,
Our voices echo, a lasting dawn.
In every heart, we find the lyrics,
In communal songs, we break the limits.

The Dance of Capitals

In a city, lights will glow,
Voices echo, here they flow.
Streets alive with tales untold,
Dreams awaken, brave and bold.

Skyscrapers sway in twilight hue,
Each window holds a point of view.
Paths converge in rhythmic stride,
Weaving stories side by side.

Bridges arch with graceful ease,
Hearts unite in gentle breeze.
Footsteps marking soft terrain,
Together dance, breaking the chain.

Cultures blend in vibrant night,
Every heartbeat feels so right.
In this waltz, we're never lost,
Embracing warmth, no matter cost.

The city sings beneath the stars,
Dancing rhythms heal the scars.
Hand in hand, we face the dawn,
In every step, a new bond drawn.

Interlinked Chords

Strings vibrating with the sound,
Harmony that knows no bound.
In the quiet, voices rise,
Creating music, hearts comprise.

Fingers dance upon the fret,
Melodies we won't forget.
Each note a thread, strength betwixt,
In this tapestry, love's mixed.

Rhythms pulse in every heart,
Unified, we play our part.
Resonating through the air,
A symphony of hope we share.

Harmony breaks through the night,
Casting shadows into light.
Every chord a bridge we make,
Creating waves, for love's sake.

Together, we compose the song,
In this space, we all belong.
Interlinked, our spirits soar,
In the music, we explore.

Waves of Togetherness

Upon the shore, the tides will rise,
Rippling echoes, soft goodbyes.
Hands entwined, we watch the sea,
In its flow, we feel so free.

With every wave, a story told,
Carried whispers, brave and bold.
Salt upon our skin, we stand,
In the current, hand in hand.

Surfing dreams, we catch the swell,
In the depths, our hearts will dwell.
Riding ripples, laughter plays,
In this dance, love's warm embrace.

High and low, the ocean's breath,
Guides us through, life and death.
In the waves, our spirits blend,
Together here, we shall transcend.

Seasons shift, the tides will wane,
But our bond will still remain.
Waves of joy and waves of pain,
In togetherness, all we gain.

Symphony of the Shared

Voices gathered, hearts align,
A symphony, so divine.
In the chorus, dreams entwined,
Echoed songs, forever bind.

Each gentle note a vivid hue,
Painting skies of sparkling blue.
Share our burdens, share the light,
In the cadence, hearts take flight.

Moments cherished, laughter bright,
In the stillness, we find might.
Together, we break the night,
Unified, we stand upright.

Filling spaces, weaving tales,
In this ocean, hope prevails.
A symphony of souls combined,
Celebrating love unconfined.

With each crescendo, hands will rise,
Melodies under starry skies.
In the music, we find peace,
A symphony that will not cease.

Interwoven Journeys

We walk together, side by side,
Paths entwined, a shared divide.
Through valleys deep and mountains high,
In every step, together we fly.

With every heartbeat, stories blend,
Old trails whisper, new ones mend.
Footprints marked on dusty ground,
In our journey, love is found.

Winds of change may twist and turn,
Yet in our hearts, the fires burn.
In silence shared, in laughter loud,
We weave our dreams, a vibrant shroud.

A tapestry of tales unfolds,
In colors rich, in hues of gold.
Together, we will face the storm,
Hand in hand, forever warm.

Fragments of a Collective Voice

In echoes soft, our voices rise,
Each note a truth, beneath the skies.
Together we blend, a symphony,
In harmony, we find the key.

Whispers carried on the breeze,
Fragments of hope, a world to seize.
Every story, every song,
Together we stand, where we belong.

Words unspoken find their grace,
In every heart, we find our place.
With each heartbeat, we create
A chorus strong, a force of fate.

In the silence, we unite,
Illuminated by shared light.
In every challenge, every choice,
We stand as one, a single voice.

Harmonies of the Heart

Beneath the stars, our spirits soar,
In gentle rhythms, we explore.
Notes of laughter, sighs of peace,
In love's embrace, we find release.

Melodies entwined, a sacred bond,
Across the ages, we respond.
With every heartbeat, every glance,
We dance together, lost in chance.

In quiet moments, whispers sound,
A serenade where love is found.
Each pulse a promise, strong and true,
In every note, I find you too.

Together in the symphony,
A tapestry of you and me.
In the silence, let love start,
Creating ours, harmonies of the heart.

The Pulse of Kinship

In gatherings bright, our laughter rings,
Echoes of joy, the warmth it brings.
Together we dance, with open hearts,
In every moment, kinship starts.

Through trials faced, we learn and grow,
In shared experiences, love will flow.
The pulse of life, a steady beat,
In every challenge, we meet defeat.

Hand in hand, we navigate,
Through joyful times and heavy weight.
The bond we share, a golden thread,
In every memory, love is fed.

Roots so deep, we stand as one,
Under the same moon, the same sun.
With every heartbeat, strong and wise,
Kinship sparks like stars in the skies.

Murmurs of Together

In whispers soft we share the night,
Secrets dance in silver light.
Hearts entwined, we find our way,
Murmurs sweet, here we shall stay.

Through laughter, tears, our stories flow,
In every touch, our spirits grow.
As shadows play on moonlit ground,
Together we are truly found.

The world may spin, yet we are still,
With every breath, our dreams fulfilled.
In gentle tides, our souls will meet,
Murmurs echo, bittersweet.

In this embrace, we hold the key,
To harmony, just you and me.
A symphony of voices blend,
Bound in love that will not end.

So let us gather, hearts so close,
In every moment, joy we chose.
Murmurs linger, soft and bright,
Together, we ignite the night.

Interharmonic Sphere

In a realm where notes unite,
Vibrations soar, pure and bright.
Each tone a thread, a path we weave,
In this sphere, we dare believe.

Celestial chords, they intertwine,
Voices rising, yours and mine.
A dance of sound, the world we make,
In harmony, we gently wake.

Echoes ripple, soft and clear,
Resonating, drawing near.
Through every pulse, our spirits blend,
In this sphere, hearts cannot bend.

Chasing rhythms, lost in time,
Melodies climb, so sublime.
With every beat, we feel alive,
In this dance, we truly thrive.

Together we create the song,
In this space, we all belong.
Interharmonic, vast and wide,
With open hearts, we take the ride.

Chiming Together

Bells resound, a joyful ring,
Echoes of love, we shall bring.
In unison, our voices blend,
Chiming softly, hearts transcend.

Through valleys deep, our laughter flies,
In every chime, the spirit sighs.
With every note, we climb so high,
Together, we touch the sky.

As echoes fade, they linger still,
In every heart, a gentle thrill.
Chiming together, old and new,
In unity, we find our true.

Resonance bright, we stand as one,
In every dusk, in every sun.
The music flows, never blurred,
Chiming together, undeterred.

Here in the sound, we're intertwined,
In every chime, your heart is mine.
Let bells ring out, a bright display,
Chiming together, come what may.

The Tuning of Kin

In the weave of family ties,
Love's sweet song forever flies.
In the moments soft and true,
The tuning of kin, me and you.

Through seasons change, we find our beat,
In every challenge, we won't retreat.
In laughter shared and sorrow's night,
We tune our hearts, igniting light.

In circles drawn, where we belong,
Each heartbeat sings a timeless song.
With threads of love, we craft our fate,
The tuning of kin, never late.

As echoes fade into the past,
In memories stitched, our bonds will last.
Through trials faced, we rise again,
In harmony, we are the same.

Together we sway, hearts aligned,
In this tapestry, love intertwined.
The tuning of kin, forever true,
In every note, it's me and you.

The Ties That Sing

In whispers soft, our secrets dwell,
Colors blend, a timeless spell.
With every note, the heartstrings pull,
Together, we're forever full.

Harmony flows, a gentle tide,
In laughter shared, we confide.
Each moment shared, a precious thread,
In the tapestry of words unsaid.

Through trials faced, we find our way,
Strength we draw from love's array.
In every song, a story we weave,
In the ties of love, we believe.

Voices rise, a chorus bright,
Carried forth into the night.
United, we conquer all fears,
In the symphony of years.

Side by side, in joy and sorrow,
Crafting dreams of a bright tomorrow.
With every chord, we together cling,
In the beauty of the ties that sing.

Notes of Affinity

Silent echoes of a gentle tune,
Underneath the silver moon.
In every glance, a spark ignites,
A world created in our sights.

Melodies flow, sweet and pure,
Joining hearts, we feel secure.
In whispered words, the truth unfolds,
With every note, a feeling holds.

Together we dance, a waltz so light,
In rhythm's embrace, we find our flight.
Hand in hand, we brave the storm,
In notes of affinity, we stay warm.

With laughter shared, the joy expands,
Forging bonds with gentle hands.
In every chord, a memory glows,
In the harmony, our love grows.

Like stars that twinkle in the night,
Each note creates a spark of light.
In perfect time, we sing our song,
In notes of affinity, we belong.

The Fabric of Voices

Woven threads of vibrant hue,
Each whisper carries something new.
In laughter loud and sorrowed sigh,
The fabric of voices we rely.

Patterns form in every phrase,
A tapestry of shared displays.
In harmony, we find our way,
Through woven dreams that brightly lay.

Echoes linger, rich and warm,
Together we weather any storm.
In resonance, our spirits soar,
The fabric binds us evermore.

Through shifting tones, we stand as one,
In every note, our triumphs spun.
In every voice, a piece remains,
In the fabric of love, no one wanes.

A chorus rises, bold and free,
Crafting memories, you and me.
Each thread a story, vibrant and true,
In the fabric of voices, I find you.

Weaving Soundscapes

In golden hues of dawn's first light,
We gather dreams, our hearts take flight.
Notes entwine like tendrils strong,
Weaving soundscapes where we belong.

Beneath the trees, a whispering breeze,
Nature sings with flowing ease.
In every sound, the world abounds,
Woven harmonies in joyful rounds.

From laughter's spark to silence deep,
In every note, our memories leap.
Crafting worlds with tender care,
Through woven sound, our souls laid bare.

With every chord, new tales unfold,
In soundscapes rich, our lives retold.
Together we dance, with spirits bold,
In the music of love, forever gold.

In twilight's glow, a serenade,
Weaving dreams that will not fade.
Each heart a note, in rhythm we find,
In weaving soundscapes, we're intertwined.

Resonant Harmonies

In twilight's glow, soft whispers call,
Nature's pulse, a unison thrall.
Each note dances, the silence breaks,
In heartbeats shared, a rhythm awakens.

Waves gently crash on shores of time,
Melodies blend in the sweet sublime.
Echoes of laughter, bright and clear,
In every harmony, you feel me near.

The stars above, they hum and sway,
A chorus bright in the dark ballet.
With every sigh, a deep embrace,
Together we find our sacred space.

In music's arms we find our way,
Guided by love, come what may.
Bound by the chords that we have spun,
In every heart, a song begun.

So let us dance as the echoes play,
In resonant harmonies, forever stay.
With you beside me, the world aligned,
In soulful tunes, our fates entwined.

Whispers in the Void

In shadows deep, where silence reigns,
A breathless hush, where nothing gains.
Yet in the stillness, secrets breathe,
Whispers linger, a soft reprieve.

Stars flicker faint in the cosmic sea,
Giving silent hymns to you and me.
In vacant spaces, dreams take flight,
Guided by beams of distant light.

Faint echoes drift in the midnight air,
Stories untold, laid bare with care.
Through silence profound, I hear your name,
In emptiness, there's warmth, not blame.

A quiet yearning, a distant song,
In the void's embrace, we both belong.
So let us wander through paths unseen,
Where whispers linger, soft and serene.

In starlit quiet, our hearts will soar,
In whispers of love, forevermore.
In the space between, we find our way,
Together in stillness, come what may.

Threads of Connection

Fine threads weave through the fabric of time,
In every touch, every word, a rhyme.
Intertwined lives, tangled yet free,
In the great tapestry, you and me.

Moments ripple like stones in a stream,
Each connection a fleeting dream.
In laughter shared, in tears we shed,
These threads hold fast, where stories are bred.

Colors blend in a spectrum bright,
Together we shimmer, a radiant light.
In every heartbeat, a message flows,
Through every distance, our love still grows.

So let us cherish these bonds divine,
In the weave of existence, your hand in mine.
With every encounter, new threads will form,
In the warmth of connection, hearts stay warm.

As seasons shift and the world turns round,
In this masterpiece, our love is found.
Through trials and joys, let's stay intertwined,
In threads of connection, eternally combined.

Convergence of Souls

Under the moon where shadows blend,
Two stories meet, and paths will tend.
In twilight's glow, we find our place,
A convergence of souls, a gentle grace.

With every glance, a spark ignites,
In the stillness, our hearts take flight.
Together we weave a destiny bright,
In the dance of the stars, we find our light.

In whispered hopes, we take the leap,
In the depth of night, our dreams we keep.
Embraced by fate that knows no end,
In love's sweet echo, around the bend.

So grab my hand, let's break the mold,
In this swirling world, our stories hold.
With every heartbeat, we merge and meld,
In this sacred space, our fears dispelled.

As dawn unfolds, we'll rise anew,
In the harmony of hearts, forever true.
In this convergence, our spirits soar,
Together, my love, forevermore.

The Sound of Unity

In the quiet of the night, we stand,
Voices merging, hand in hand.
Echoes dance through the cool breeze,
Harmony flows with perfect ease.

Every heartbeat sings a tune,
Beneath the watchful silver moon.
Together we craft a melody,
In silence, we find synergy.

Notes align in soft embrace,
Resonance fills this sacred space.
Each whisper adds to the grand score,
Unity's sound forevermore.

When troubles rise and shadows fall,
We lift each other, hear the call.
In every note, our spirits soar,
The sound of us forevermore.

Let the music ring so true,
In every color, every hue.
With every chord, our love ignites,
A symphony that feels just right.

Cadence of the Cosmos

Stars above in swirling grace,
Each one shines, a warm embrace.
With every blink, they tell a tale,
Of cosmic bonds that never pale.

Galaxies spin in rhythmic dance,
Infinite wonders in every glance.
Time and space intertwine as one,
Cradling secrets of the sun.

Planets turn with perfect rhyme,
The universe keeps perfect time.
Gravity pulls; we feel the tug,
In starlit paths, we're all snug.

Comets streak with brilliant light,
Marking moments in the night.
The cadence of the cosmos sings,
In every breath, creation brings.

In this vast and endless dome,
Together we find our place, our home.
With every heartbeat, love will grow,
In the universe's endless flow.

Reflections of Togetherness

In quiet moments, side by side,
Mirrored souls, we won't divide.
Every glance a story told,
In this bond, we find our gold.

Through the storms and sunny days,
In every laugh and gentle phrase,
We build our world in quiet trust,
In unity, we strongly rust.

Shared dreams dance like morning light,
Together, we shine, oh so bright.
In every challenge that we face,
We lift each other, find our place.

Memories formed in shared embrace,
Time will never erase our grace.
Reflections tell of love so pure,
In togetherness, we are secure.

With every heartbeat, we will grow,
In a garden that we sow.
The beauty found in you and me,
Is the essence of our unity.

The Symphony of Us

In the orchestra of life, we play,
Different instruments every day.
Together we create a song,
In every note, we will belong.

Strings and winds blend in delight,
Creating magic, pure and bright.
The rhythm sways in gentle tide,
With every heartbeat, side by side.

Melodies rise in sweet refrain,
In joy and sorrow, love remains.
The symphony intertwines our hearts,
In perfect harmony, never parts.

Every crescendo, every fall,
Tells the story of us all.
In this dance, we find our way,
Guided by love, come what may.

Let the world hear our tune,
In every morning, every noon.
The symphony of us will soar,
An everlasting, cherished score.

Harmonious Threads

In soft whispers, colors blend,
Each note a stroke of gentle grace,
Weaving tales that time does send,
A tapestry of love's embrace.

From vibrant dreams, our spirits soar,
Bound by threads that interlace,
Together we create and explore,
In every heart, a sacred space.

With every laugh, a bond grows strong,
Echoes of joy in every heart,
In unity, we find our song,
A masterpiece, a work of art.

Through valleys deep and mountains wide,
Together on this journey grand,
We walk with faith, not fear or pride,
In every step, we understand.

So let us stitch our lives as one,
In vibrant hues of shared intent,
With open hearts, we've just begun,
Creating moments heaven-sent.

Chorus of the Collective

Voices rise in sweet refrain,
Together we create a song,
In harmony, we feel no pain,
Through every note, we all belong.

Hands are lifted, spirits high,
Each heartbeat syncs, an endless beat,
Underneath this vast, warm sky,
Our chorus makes the world complete.

Melodies of hope arise,
Every voice a precious thread,
Boundless dreams that reach the skies,
In this unity, we are led.

With rhythms strong, we dance as one,
Through valleys deep, to peaks so bright,
The journey shared, no need to run,
Together, we find true delight.

In moments fleeting, we embrace,
This chorus echoes evermore,
Our hearts, a home, our sacred space,
In love's reflection, we restore.

Fusion of Voices

When voices blend in gentle grace,
A symphony of dreams takes flight,
From every heart, a sacred place,
Where shadows fade, and souls ignite.

In whispers soft, the stories weave,
Uniting past and future bright,
Each truth laid bare, we dare believe,
Together, we embrace the light.

With colored notes, we paint the air,
A canvas vast, both bold and true,
In every sound, a loving care,
As melodies rise, our spirits grew.

We dance to echoes of the night,
In every rhythm, hearts align,
The fusion bold, a pure delight,
In every moment, love will shine.

So let us sing, no fear, no fight,
In perfect harmony, we stand,
Together, in this sacred light,
A fusion formed by grace's hand.

Pulses of Tranquility

In quiet moments, peace unfolds,
A gentle drum, a heart's soft beat,
With each pulse, a story told,
In silence found, our spirits meet.

The world outside may rush and roar,
Yet in our souls, a calm reside,
We breathe in deep, and we restore,
In tranquil waves, our fears subside.

Flowing like rivers, soft and free,
The pulse of nature guides our way,
In every breath, a clarity,
As stars above begin to sway.

With open hearts, the peace we seek,
A bond unbroken, ever strong,
In whispers shared, no need to speak,
Together, we will sing our song.

So let us cherish each heartbeat,
In tranquil moments, there we find,
The pulse of life, a rare retreat,
In harmony, our souls entwined.

Interlaced Souls

In the gentle breeze we meet,
Two hearts in rhythm, so sweet.
Our laughter dances in the air,
Threads of life, woven with care.

With whispered dreams, we intertwine,
Echoes of love, pure and divine.
In shadows cast, we find our way,
Together, night blends into day.

The world fades, time stands still,
Connected by a quiet thrill.
In every glance, a spark ignites,
Guiding us through starry nights.

Hands entwined, we walk the path,
Fading doubts, we chase the laugh.
In silence shared, solace found,
Two souls in unity, profound.

With every heartbeat, we align,
Two journeys merge, a sacred sign.
In this embrace, we come alive,
Interlaced souls, forever thrive.

Cadence of Common Ground

In the rhythm of shared embrace,
We find our steps, a gentle pace.
Voices blend in soft refrain,
A harmony, unbroken chain.

Beneath the sky, our dreams take flight,
Guided by the stars so bright.
In every sigh, a bond we weave,
Together stronger, we believe.

Laughter spills like morning dew,
In every smile, a world anew.
Each heartbeat keeping time so sound,
In unity, we are found.

With open hearts, we face the dawn,
In common ground, we all belong.
A melody that never fades,
In shared moments, love cascades.

As seasons change, we hold on tight,
In the cadence of day and night.
With every breath, we speak our truth,
In joyful echoes, we find our youth.

The Language of Together

In whispers soft, we find a way,
Words unspoken, where hearts sway.
A glance exchanged, a knowing light,
In silence shared, we take flight.

Threads of laughter, colors bright,
Painting moments, pure delight.
With every hug, we bridge the space,
In this embrace, we find our place.

Through trials faced, we stand as one,
In the warmth of each rising sun.
With hands held tight, we face the storm,
In love's embrace, we are reborn.

Every heartbeat, a sacred tale,
In the language of love, we prevail.
With every step, we walk the line,
In the quest for joy, we intertwine.

In the dance of life, we move as one,
In this journey, we have begun.
Together we speak what words cannot,
In the language of love, we are caught.

Spheres of Affinity

In circles drawn by fate's design,
We orbit close, our hearts align.
Through every twist, through every turn,
In shared passion, forever burn.

With every glance, a spark ignites,
In realms of dreams, we scale new heights.
Our spirits soar like birds in flight,
Guided by love's radiant light.

Together, we dance on cosmic waves,
In the rhythm of life, our path engraves.
With every step, the universe sighs,
In spheres of affinity, love never dies.

As seasons blend, we flow like streams,
In the fabric of time, we weave our dreams.
With open arms, we greet the dawn,
In this tapestry, heartstrings drawn.

With hearts united, we face the night,
In the dance of souls, everything feels right.
Through cosmic tides, we navigate,
In spheres of affinity, we create.

Whispers of Harmony

In the stillness, soft echoes glide,
Gentle breezes, stars collide.
Nature's voice in quiet song,
Binding hearts that feel so strong.

Through the leaves, a secret shared,
Hope in whispers, deeply cared.
Harmony dances in the night,
Guided by the silver light.

Each heartbeat syncs, a tender thread,
Affection blooms where love is spread.
Together we'll find endless grace,
In every smile, in every embrace.

Silent moments, hand in hand,
In perfect peace, together we stand.
Lifting spirits, weaving dreams,
In unity, nothing's as it seems.

As we wander, paths entwine,
With every breath, your heart is mine.
In whispers soft, our souls align,
In the night, forever shine.

Resonant Threads

Threads of laughter, woven bright,
In every heart, a spark ignites.
We spin the tales of days gone by,
In every whisper, love's sweet sigh.

Through stormy skies, we find our way,
Hand in hand, come what may.
A tapestry of hopes and dreams,
United now, or so it seems.

Voices blend in colors bold,
In every story, warmth unfolds.
With every note, we rise and soar,
Together always, forevermore.

Moments shared, no need for words,
In silence, harmony is heard.
Resonant threads of joy and pain,
We dance through sunshine, through the rain.

Together in this endless flow,
Hearts aligned, we ebb and glow.
With every step, in tune we tread,
In life's grand fabric, we are led.

Voices in Synchrony

In the dawn, our voices rise,
Melodies weave 'neath the skies.
Echoes intertwine and blend,
In perfect rhythm, hearts ascend.

Together we share dreams so bright,
In every glance, a hint of light.
Lifting spirits, soaring high,
In the harmony, we fly.

Silken tones in evening's glow,
Each whisper carries love's soft flow.
Chords of laughter, pulses meet,
In this symphony, life's sweet beat.

As we march through time's embrace,
Every step, a sacred space.
Voices rise and gently sway,
In synchrony, we greet the day.

Through shadows deep, we'll find our way,
In unity, forever stay.
Echoes of love, bright and true,
In voices soft, I find you.

Melodies of Togetherness

Under starlight, we softly hum,
Melodies sweet, the night's become.
Hands entwined, a tender grace,
In every note, we find our place.

Across fields of dreams, we wander free,
Nature sings in harmony.
In every step, the music flows,
A dance of joy, as friendship grows.

The gentle strum of hearts in tune,
Beneath the watchful, silver moon.
Together, we shape the night's soft song,
In melodies where we belong.

With every laugh, a brighter sound,
In that magic, love is found.
In shared moments, spirits lift,
Together, life's the greatest gift.

So let us cherish, day by day,
This symphony in every way.
In harmony, our hearts combine,
In melodies, forever shine.

Notes from a Shared Path

Along the winding road we tread,
With whispers soft and hearts un-led.
Our footsteps blend, a gentle song,
In harmony, we both belong.

Each bend reveals a truth anew,
As shadows dance in morning dew.
We share the light, we share the dark,
Illuminating every spark.

Through laughter's echoes, tears we sow,
In silence deep, our spirits grow.
Together facing storms we find,
A bond unbreakable, lovingly blind.

With every step, a chance to learn,
Within our hearts, the embers burn.
We map the stars, both near and far,
Guided always by who we are.

In fading dusk, as night descends,
The path is clear; our journey bends.
We'll trace the dreams, the hopes we weave,
In every breath, we still believe.

Collectively Speaking

Words gather 'round like autumn leaves,
In whispers shared, the heart believes.
Our voices rise, a vibrant blend,
United, whole, we shall transcend.

From diverse shades, a canvas bright,
Creating stories, taking flight.
Through every laugh and every sigh,
Together we shall reach the sky.

In echoes rich, our truths align,
A tapestry from yours and mine.
We craft a world, bold and vast,
In this moment, we are cast.

Our hearts a chorus, strong and clear,
Each note, a tribute to all we steer.
Through storms of doubt, we'll navigate,
In unity, we find our fate.

Each voice a spark, igniting change,
In shared intent, we rearrange.
Together, lifting heavy hearts,
In every word, new hope imparts.

The Sound of Togetherness

In the still of morning's light,
We wake to warmth, a pure delight.
The sound of laughter fills the air,
A melody, beyond compare.

With every beat, our hearts engage,
A symphony upon life's stage.
Through highs and lows, the notes persist,
A harmony we can't resist.

From whispered dreams to shouts of glee,
In every moment, you and me.
The rhythm swells, each pulse a sign,
In this dance, our souls entwine.

In quiet nights, under the stars,
We share our hopes, we mend our scars.
The sound of unity rings clear,
A vow of love for all to hear.

As seasons change and time moves fast,
We cherish moments that are cast.
In every laugh, every embrace,
The sound of togetherness we trace.

Interlude of Unity

In the pause between each breath,
We find our peace, life's gentle heft.
An interlude, a soft refrain,
Where love transcends both joy and pain.

Together here, our spirits blend,
In quiet whispers, hearts we send.
The silence speaks, a sacred space,
Where souls, in trust, find their place.

In every glance, a world revealed,
Through shared experience, hearts are healed.
In unity, we rise and stand,
A tapestry woven hand in hand.

In moments brief, the magic's found,
In quietude, our thoughts resound.
This interlude, a sacred song,
Where all of us can feel we belong.

No need for words, just presence shared,
In stillness deep, we're unprepared.
Yet in that hush, a bond takes flight,
An interlude of pure delight.

Tapestry of Echoes

Whispers weave through twilight's shade,
Threads of silver softly laid.
Each note lingers, softly spun,
In the glow of setting sun.

Memories dance on gentle winds,
Carried forth where longing begins.
Hearts entwined in shadow's grasp,
Fleeting moments, time's sweet clasp.

Silent songs in twilight speak,
In the hush, our voices seek.
The fabric of our souls collide,
In echoes where our hopes abide.

Stars above in silence gleam,
Reflecting dreams in silver stream.
A tapestry of nights unfurls,
In the bonds of hidden worlds.

Yet in the night, a truth is told,
In every thread, a heart of gold.
Through every echo, we find grace,
A cherished song, a timeless space.

United in Reverberation

Voices rise, a vibrant swell,
In harmony, our stories dwell.
Like rivers flowing, bold and bright,
Together we ignite the night.

Hands held tight, our spirits soar,
Echoing dreams that we explore.
A symphony of hearts combined,
In reverberation, love defined.

Each heartbeat joins a rhythmic call,
In unity, we rise or fall.
A dance of shadows, light, and sound,
In this embrace, our truth is found.

Step by step, we walk as one,
Beneath the moon, beneath the sun.
Resonating through the night,
In every pulse, we feel the light.

Together forged, our voices blend,
In every note, love has no end.
United we stand, forever strong,
In reverberation, we belong.

Chorus of Kindred Spirits

In quiet moments, hearts align,
A gentle hum, a sacred sign.
Kindred spirits draw so near,
In the chorus, love is clear.

Through laughter shared and tears we shed,
In every word, our souls are fed.
Voices rise like morning light,
In a harmony, pure and bright.

With every chord, we weave our tale,
In whispered winds, we set our sail.
Echoes blend in sweet refrain,
Finding peace amidst the pain.

In this song, we find our way,
Through the shadows, into the day.
Together, we will always sing,
A chorus of what love can bring.

With open hearts, we mend and grow,
In every note, a chance to glow.
Symphony of souls entwined,
In kindred spirits, love defined.

Euphonic Embrace

In dawn's first light, a melody,
Softly rising, wild and free.
Notes like petals, fresh and bright,
In euphonic waves, take flight.

Each breath a song, a subtle grace,
In harmony, we find our place.
The world unfolds, a canvas wide,
In music's arms, our hopes abide.

Together lost in rhythm's sway,
In sweet embrace, we drift away.
Echoes linger, soft and true,
In the silence, I find you.

With whispered dreams and laughter's cheer,
We share our secrets, drawing near.
Euphonic moments, tender, sweet,
In our hearts, the world's complete.

Time stands still as voices meld,
In this embrace, our souls are held.
As notes entwine, the spirit soars,
In perfect balance, love restores.

Echoes of Shared Dreams

Beneath the stars we shared a glance,
Whispers of hope in twilight's dance.
Together we wandered, hand in hand,
Carving our futures, a love so grand.

In silent moments, hearts align,
Echoes of laughter, soft and divine.
With every heartbeat, a promise made,
In the tapestry of dreams, we stayed.

Time may pass, but we'll remain,
In fleeting dreams, love's sweet refrain.
Through every storm, we'll journey far,
Guided always by our shared star.

When shadows fall and doubts arise,
We'll lift each other towards the skies.
For in our souls, the dream persists,
A love like ours, one will always miss.

As echoes fade, we'll find our way,
In the light of love, come what may.
Together we soar, our spirits free,
In the realm of dreams, just you and me.

Chords of the Heart

Strumming softly, the strings entwine,
In every note, your heart is mine.
Melodies linger, sweetly they play,
Guiding our souls through night and day.

Each heartbeat resonates with grace,
A harmony found in your embrace.
In every silence, a song is born,
A symphony where true love's worn.

Through trials faced, our music swells,
With chords of trust, our spirit dwells.
In whispers shared beneath the stars,
Resounding love, no distance mars.

Together we'll write our timeless score,
In every measure, we explore.
A duet played with hands and heart,
From this world, we'll never part.

As long as life and music flow,
Through every melody, our love will grow.
With every strum, a promise we keep,
In chords of heart, our dreams run deep.

Interlaced Melodies

In the garden of sound, we intertwine,
Your laughter dances, a sweet design.
In whispered verses, our stories blend,
Melodies mingling, a heart to mend.

Notes drift gently on evening air,
With every harmony, we find our care.
As rhythms pulse in perfect time,
Together we carve our love in rhyme.

In vibrant colors, the music plays,
A canvas painted with love's warm rays.
Through every measure, hand in hand,
We build our dreams upon this land.

With each crescendo, our spirits soar,
Interlaced melodies, forever more.
In every chorus, a bond so tight,
Together we blaze, a radiant light.

As songs fade softly into the night,
We'll carry our tune, forever bright.
In the echoes of time, we'll find our place,
Interlaced melodies, woven with grace.

Voices in Accord

In the quiet hush, our voices rise,
A chorus woven beneath the skies.
With every word, our dreams take flight,
Together we sing, igniting the night.

From distant shores, we find our song,
In unity's strength, we'll all belong.
Harmony flows through hearts so true,
As we create the world anew.

Through every sorrow, through every cheer,
Our voices meld, banishing fear.
In the symphony of life we find,
A radiant bond that ties each mind.

When the world feels heavy, still we sing,
In voices of love, we find our spring.
A melody shared can heal the heart,
In this grand symphony, we'll never part.

Together we stand, together we thrive,
With voices in accord, we come alive.
In every harmony, journeys begin,
Voices in accord, our souls will win.

The Pulse of Unity

In the heart of the crowd, we stand,
Voices blend like grains of sand.
Each beat a bond, a shared embrace,
Together we forge, a sacred space.

Hands raised high in a silent cheer,
Every heartbeat loud and clear.
Echoing dreams in the twilight glow,
In unity's warmth, we all grow.

Threads of laughter weave the night,
Dancing shadows, wings in flight.
A tapestry rich with stories told,
The pulse of unity, brave and bold.

As dawn approaches, we still remain,
Bound by joy, not by pain.
In every smile, in every tear,
We pulse as one, year after year.

From mountain peaks to ocean's shore,
Our spirits rise, forevermore.
Together we stand, a force sublime,
In the pulse of unity, we find our rhyme.

Infinite Reverberations

Whispers echo through the night,
Carried softly, pure delight.
In every corner, shadows play,
Infinite sounds that never sway.

A breeze that sings with ancient grace,
Filling the air, a warm embrace.
Each note a ripple, ever free,
Reverberations, our harmony.

Time stretches long, it bends and sways,
In twilight's glow, forever stays.
The past and future, mingled sound,
In infinite echoes, love is found.

Every heartbeat's gentle thrum,
The pulse of echoes, we become.
In reverberations, we create,
A melody that won't abate.

When silence falls, we still can hear,
Whispers of hope, forever near.
In every breath, the world aligns,
Infinite reverberations, heart entwined.

Phonetic Ties

Words unspoken dance around,
In silence, a deeper sound.
Phonetic ties that bind us close,
In every whisper, love engrossed.

Through starlit nights, we find our way,
In every sound, a soft ballet.
The language of hearts, it resonates,
Phonetic ties that fate creates.

Notes that linger in the air,
Carrying dreams, striping despair.
In every echo, our spirits rise,
Phonetic whispers, no goodbyes.

Stories woven in the night,
Crafted softly, pure delight.
Words like threads, they intertwine,
Phonetic ties, forever shine.

With every laugh, with every tear,
In phonetics, we adhere.
In the fabric of love, we find,
Phonetic ties that weave mankind.

Symphonic Whispers

Softly, gently, music flows,
In the stillness, passion grows.
With every note, an echo sings,
Symphonic whispers, timeless things.

A dance of shadows, light and dark,
In every silence, there's a spark.
Harmony found in fleeting sighs,
Symphonic whispers, never die.

Through the ages, melodies roam,
In every heart, they find a home.
Threading through the fabric sweet,
Symphonic whispers, life's heartbeat.

Amidst the chaos, still they play,
Guiding lost souls along the way.
In every moment, rich and rare,
Symphonic whispers soothe our care.

As the night yields to the dawn,
In whispered songs, we are reborn.
With every breath, we softly sound,
Symphonic whispers all around.

Resonant Pathways

In twilight's glow we wander slow,
Through whispers of the pines that flow.
Each step a note in nature's song,
A melody where hearts belong.

The rivers hum with tales unspun,
While shadows dance as daylight's done.
In echoes soft, our spirits meet,
On pathways long, we find our feet.

The stars align in silent praise,
Guiding us through the winding maze.
Each twist and turn, a chance to grow,
In life's vast canvas, colors glow.

Through valleys deep and mountains high,
The breeze invites a gentle sigh.
In harmony our dreams take flight,
A tapestry of heart and light.

So take my hand and walk with me,
Resonance blooms in unity.
Together we will weave our song,
In perfect sync, where we belong.

Entwined Echoes

In the night, our voices blend,
Creating worlds that never end.
Each echo carries dreams anew,
Entwined in paths we once both knew.

The tales of old in shadows sigh,
Weaving stories, as time slips by.
In vibrant hues our hearts unite,
A chorus rising in the light.

With every laugh, a bond we forge,
Through every tear, a love that roars.
In every moment, memories trace,
Entwined echoes in time and space.

So listen close, the whispers call,
A guiding force that keeps us whole.
In every heartbeat, there's a sign,
Entwined echoes, yours and mine.

Voice of the Collective

In every hush, the voices rise,
A symphony beneath the skies.
Together strong, we make our stand,
Crafting dreams with gentle hands.

With every heartbeat, we connect,
In unity, we reflect.
The strength found in the many faces,
In harmony, our hope embraces.

Through stormy nights and sunny days,
We share the load in countless ways.
From each of us, a story shared,
In the collective, we are bared.

Our laughter rings, our sorrows shared,
The voice of life, forever dared.
In the tapestry of voices bright,
We sing together, side by side.

So raise your voice, let it resound,
In every heart, let love abound.
With each new dawn, we'll strive to be,
The voice of the collective, fiercely free.

The Fabric of Connection

In threads of gold, our stories lie,
Woven tight as time goes by.
Each shared moment, a stitch defined,
The fabric of love intertwined.

Through laughter light and whispers soft,
We build a world, drifting aloft.
In each embrace, a warmth bestowed,
The fabric of connection glowed.

With every heartbeat, we create,
Designs of fate that resonate.
From every tear and every smile,
Our tapestry spans every mile.

Through trials faced and victories grand,
The threads unite, hand in hand.
In colors bold, our spirits dance,
The fabric of connection, our chance.

So hold it close, this precious weave,
In love and trust, we will believe.
Together we will stitch our dreams,
In the fabric of connection, life gleams.

Collective Crescendo

In fields of voices, we unite,
Threads of harmony take flight.
Together, we weave a tale,
Rising strong, we shall not fail.

Chords of dreaming, soft yet bold,
Tales of warmth in whispers told.
Every note a heart's embrace,
In this moment, we find grace.

Hearts a-beating, hands entwined,
Lost in rhythm, intertwined.
With a pulse that guides our way,
We stand firm, come what may.

Voices swell like spring's sweet breeze,
A chorus dances through the trees.
Bound by love, we sing as one,
Beneath the moon, beneath the sun.

In this crescendo, we belong,
Together, we are ever strong.
Echoes linger in the night,
A symphony of pure delight.

Waves of Resonance

Gentle whispers on the shore,
Tides of sound forever more.
Each wave carries a silent song,
Drawing us to where we belong.

Ripples dance upon the sea,
In their depths, we find the key.
Harmony beneath the sun,
Awakening everyone.

Shores collide in vibrant hues,
Nature's canvas, filled with muse.
Rolling waves that ebb and flow,
Resonating deep below.

In the ocean's vast embrace,
Time stands still in this sweet space.
Listen close, the waves will tell,
Secrets of the ocean's spell.

With every splash, our spirits rise,
Carried forth through endless skies.
Waves of resonance intertwine,
Crafting echoes pure and fine.

Bridges Through Sound

Whispers traverse the unseen way,
Building bridges, day by day.
Notes and rhythms weave their thread,
From hearts to hearts, the sound is spread.

In each echo, laughter rings,
Connections born from simple things.
Through the silence, voices grow,
Sparks of joy begin to flow.

Harmony beckons, a guiding light,
From shadows deep, we take our flight.
Crafting pathways through the air,
Together, we rise without a care.

Each melody a step we take,
In this dance, our souls awake.
Across the distance, hands will meet,
In every beat, the world's heartbeat.

In the symphony, we find our place,
Joined in song, a warm embrace.
Bridges built from love profound,
Together in this magic sound.

Timeless Echoes

In caverns deep, the echoes call,
Whispers of the past enthrall.
Memories carved in rocks so old,
Tales of life, forever told.

Each note a flicker of what once was,
A dance of time, without a pause.
Through frozen moments, we explore,
Footsteps echo evermore.

Vibrations ripple through the ages,
In each sound, history engages.
From the mountain to the sea,
Timeless echoes call to me.

In shadows cast by ancient light,
We search for meaning, day and night.
Each echo whispers, "You are free,"
Unlocking doors to memory.

As we journey, may we find,
Eternal rhythms, intertwined.
In echoes deep, our stories blend,
A symphony that will not end.

Chords of Connection

In the silence, whispers weave,
Threads of bond that we believe.
Hands entwined, hearts align,
Melodies of joy combine.

Every note a pulse anew,
Rhythms dance, like morning dew.
Echoed laughter fills the air,
Crafting dreams for us to share.

In the harmony, we find grace,
United steps in every space.
Tuning hearts to life's refrain,
Together through the joy and pain.

With each strum, our spirits soar,
In this song, we are much more.
Voices rise, the world will see,
The strength in our unity.

Let the chords forever blend,
In this journey, we transcend.
Through the echoes of our trust,
In connection, love is a must.

Reflections in Unison

In the mirror of our eyes,
Shared visions spark, and dreams arise.
Together we dance in the light,
Adapting shadows, holding tight.

Every glance a story told,
As we weave our hearts of gold.
In each moment, time stands still,
Reflections echo, we fulfill.

Kaleidoscope of hopes we share,
Colors blend in the open air.
With every heartbeat, we belong,
In this life, we write our song.

Through the laughter and the tears,
Unison silences our fears.
In harmony, we rise anew,
Together, strong, through and through.

In the tapestry of dreams we share,
Reflections shine; we're everywhere.
In this bond, our souls align,
Together, dear, you are my sign.

The Sound of Solidarity

In the distance, voices blend,
Harmony as we transcend.
In the struggle, strength we find,
Together, one, forever kind.

With every step, we pave the way,
Side by side, come what may.
Through the storms, we stand our ground,
In the silence, love resounds.

Echoed calls of brave hearts throng,
In this fight, we all belong.
Symphonies of courage rise,
In solidarity, we are wise.

From every corner, hands are raised,
In our unity, we are praised.
With one voice, we softly plead,
Together we plant the seed.

In the chorus, hope takes flight,
Guiding us into the night.
In this sound, we find our way,
Solidarity shall stay.

Symphony of Shared Dreams

Under starlight, wishes gleam,
In our hearts, a shared dream.
Notes of hope, whispering bright,
Together we'll chase the light.

In the twilight, we will sing,
Celebrating all that love brings.
Rhythms of life sync in tune,
Creating magic 'neath the moon.

In each heartbeat, visions spark,
Illuminating paths from dark.
With each chorus, we unite,
In this symphony, we ignite.

Every dream a precious thread,
Woven with the words unsaid.
With our voices, strong and clear,
We'll compose what we hold dear.

As we gather, hopes abide,
In this journey, love our guide.
With each moment, we will see,
This symphony sets us free.

Resonance in Community

In the heart of the square, they gather near,
Voices intertwine, a chorus sincere.
Echoes of laughter, stories unfold,
A tapestry woven in threads of gold.

Hands held together, strength in the bond,
In unity's embrace, they wander beyond.
Each face a chapter, each smile a light,
Creating a world where all hearts ignite.

From the young to the old, dreams take flight,
Together they rise, sharing their sight.
In shadows and sun, the ties are reinforced,
With whispers of hope, they stay the course.

In seasons of change, through joy and pain,
They dance in the rain, they flourish again.
Through kindness and love, they carve their way,
In the pulse of the community, forever they stay.

A melody sung, each note gently played,
In the symphony of life, none are dismayed.
Resonance in harmony, hearts intertwine,
In the echo of togetherness, spirits align.

Awakened Serenade

Beneath the canopy, the morning breaks,
Birds chirp a tune, the world awakes.
Sunlight cascades, a gentle caress,
Nature sings softly, in sweet impress.

Gentle whispers flow through the trees,
Carrying secrets on the warm breeze.
A harmonized dance of earth and sky,
Inviting the dreamers to spread their wings high.

In the still of the dawn, reflections arise,
The calmness envelops, where silence lies.
With every heartbeat, music takes flight,
Awakened serenade, painting the light.

Voices of the past call to the soul,
Guiding the spirit, making it whole.
In moments of stillness, we find our way,
In rhythm and rhyme, we long to stay.

As twilight descends, the stars softly gleam,
The universe whispers, a beautiful dream.
Together we stand, in awe of the night,
Awakened serenade, hearts shining bright.

Undercurrents of Togetherness

In the ripples of time, connections are cast,
Soaked in the essence of moments that last.
Beneath the surface, where feelings run deep,
Undercurrents flow, a promise to keep.

Through laughter and tears, bonds intertwine,
Navigating currents, hearts align.
In the fabric of life, woven with grace,
Together, they journey, a sacred space.

The tide pulls gently, the waves softly roll,
In the depths of the sea lies a shared soul.
With every encounter, the world expands,
In the dance of togetherness, unity stands.

Where shadows may linger, light starts to play,
Hand in hand, they find their way.
Through storms and calm, resilience will bloom,
Undercurrents of warmth dispel all the gloom.

In whispers of love, the currents will sing,
Carrying tales of the joy they bring.
Together they flourish, their spirits unite,
In the ocean of togetherness, hearts take flight.

Melodies Through Time

In the echoes of ages, a song unfolds,
Whispers of wisdom, the past gently holds.
Melodies linger, weaving through space,
Timeless and pure, a warm embrace.

With every heartbeat, a rhythm resounds,
Tracing the journey, where history bounds.
In the dance of the ages, tales are spun,
Melodies of laughter, of battles won.

Through the corridors of time, spirits ignite,
Carving their legacy, burning bright.
In notes of remembrance, connections thrive,
Singing the stories that keep us alive.

A symphony echoes, both distant and near,
Binding the moments, both happy and clear.
In every refrain, hope glimmers anew,
Melodies through time, always in view.

Together we treasure what beats in our chest,
The song of existence, a beautiful quest.
In the harmony shared, we find our way,
Melodies through time, forever will stay.

9 781805 605171